1

Gl Douglas Haig

History Through Poetry

World War I

Paul Dowswell

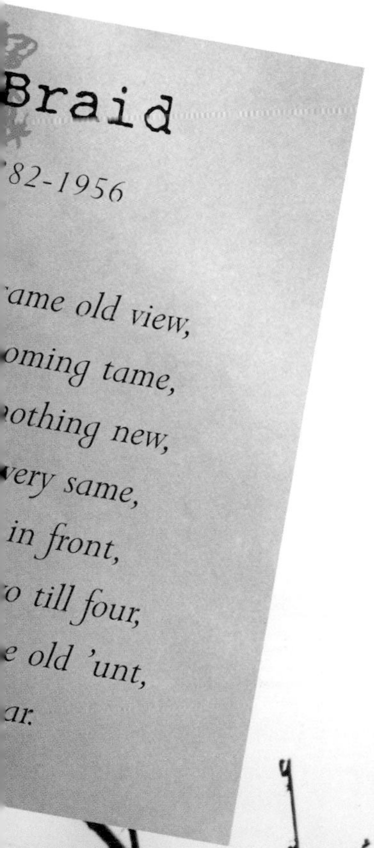
Braid
'82-1956
'ame old view,
oming tame,
othing new,
very same,
in front,
o till four,
e old 'unt,
ar.

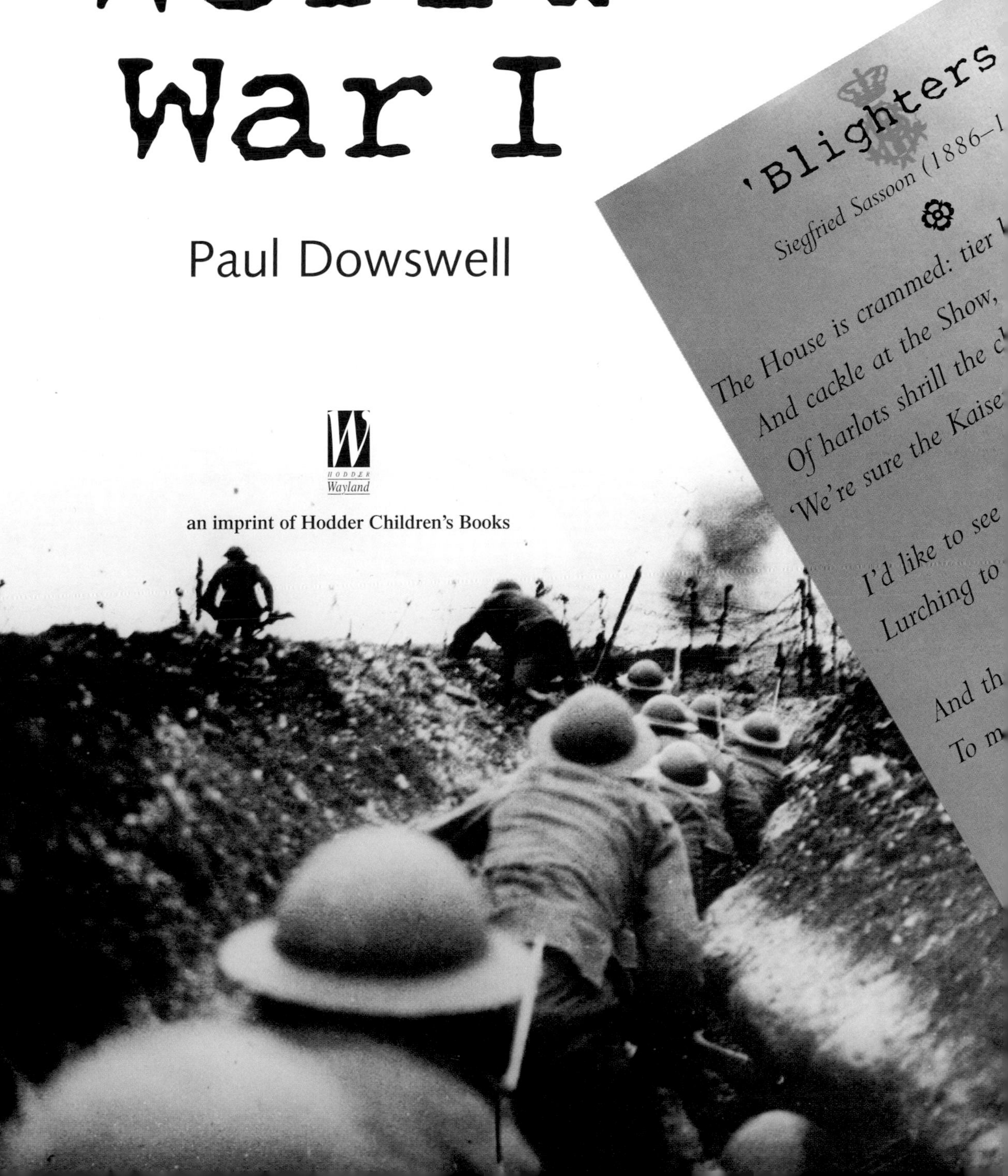
'Blighters
Siegfried Sassoon (1886–1
The House is crammed: tier
And cackle at the Show,
Of harlots shrill the c
'We're sure the Kaise
I'd like to see
Lurching to
And th
To m

Hodder Wayland

an imprint of Hodder Children's Books

History Through Poetry
Tudors
Victorians
World War I
World War II

Commissioning Editor: Alex Woolf
Editor: Jonathan Ingoldby
Designer: Simon Borrough
Cover Concept: Peta Morey

Published in Great Britain in 2001 by Hodder Wayland, an imprint of Hodder Children's Books

British Library Cataloguing in Publication Data
Dowswell, Paul
World War I. – (History Through Poetry)
1.English poetry – 20th century – Juvenile literature
2.World War, 1914-1918 – Juvenile literature
I.Title
940.3

ISBN 0 7502 3593 4

Printed in Hong Kong by Wing King Tong

Hodder Children's Books
A division of Hodder Headline Limited
338 Euston Road, London, NW1 3BH

Cover and Decorative Pictures:
The cover shows an army jacket with World War I medals, a standard-issue stationery wallet with envelopes and a fountain pen (all courtesy of the Imperial War Museum); a diary, a pocket-watch and a photograph of an army officer (all courtesy of Jonathan Ingoldby). The pictures that appear on the left-hand pages of the book are a fountain pen (p. 4); a pin badge (p. 6); a pocket watch (p. 8) (courtesy of Jonathan Ingoldby); an engraved cigarette case (p. 10); an embroidered image of Douglas Haig (p. 12); two lighters made from shell cases (p. 14); an army issue lantern (p. 16); a camera and case (p. 18); an army issue tin mug (p. 20); a model aeroplane made from bullet metal (p. 22); a pen, stationery wallet and envelopes (p. 24); World War I medals (p. 26) (all courtesy of the Imperial War Museum unless otherwise stated). All objects date from the period.

Special thanks are due to Allan Jefferies, Department of Exhibits and Firearms, Imperial War Museum.

Picture Acknowledgements
The publishers would like to thank the following for permission to reproduce their pictures: Hulton Getty 27; Imperial War Museum/Hodder Wayland Picture Library 7 (bottom), 9 (top), 15 (top), 19 (top); Peter Newark's Military Pictures 5, 7 (top), 15 (bottom), 17, 21 (bottom), 23 (top), 25; Popperfoto 11 (bottom), 13 (top), 29 (top); Topham Picturepoint 9 (bottom), 11 (top), 13 (bottom), 19 (bottom), 21 (top), 23 (bottom), 29 (bottom).

Poetry Acknowledgements
The publishers are grateful to the following for permission to reproduce copyright material:

Barbara Levy Literary Agency (Siegfried Sassoon, 'Blighters' and 'Reconciliation', copyright Siegfried Sassoon by kind permission of George Sassoon); Curtis Brown Ltd, London (A.A. Milne, 'Gold Braid' from *The Sunny Side*, copyright under the Berne Convention, reproduced by permission); Macmillan Publishers Ltd (J.C. Squire, 'God Heard the Embattled Nations'; Wilfrid Wilson Gibson, 'Troopship: Mid-Atlantic'); A.P. Watt Ltd on behalf of Michael B. Yeats (W.B. Yeats, 'An Irish Airman Foresees His Death').

'Sturmangriff' ('Charge') by August Stramm was translated by Jeremy Alder; 'Les Soliloques du Soldat' ('The Soldier's Soliloquies, I') by Marc De Larreguy De Civrieux was translated by D.D.R. Owen.

Every effort has been made to trace the copyright holders of material reproduced in this book. Any rights not acknowledged here will be acknowledged in subsequent printings if notice is given to the publisher.

CONTENTS

CAUSES OF THE WAR

Happy is England Now

John Freeman (1880–1929)

Happy is England in the brave that die
For wrongs not hers and wrongs so sternly hers;
Happy in those that give, give, and endure
The pain that never the new years may cure;
Happy in all her dark woods, green fields, towns,
Her hills and rivers and her chafing sea.

. . . happiest is England now
In those that fight, and watch with pride and tears.
(1914)

sternly
In the context of the poem, the word means unquestionably, or without a doubt.

endure
To suffer something without giving up.

chafing
Rubbing against. The poet is referring to the sea which completely surrounds the border of Britain.

This is an extract from a patriotic poem written in 1914 at the outbreak of World War I. Here, the verse begins by boldly declaring that Britain is glad to send its soldiers to die in battle, because they are fighting a just cause. It also suggests, in the phrase, 'wrongs so sternly hers', that Britain too bears responsibility for the circumstances that have led to war. The poem acknowledges that the war will bring grief, but its description of the English landscape is intended to evoke pride in the reader, and suggest that the sacrifice to come will be worthwhile.

World War I, also known as the Great War, lasted from 1914 to 1918. It was the first 'modern' war. There were tanks, aeroplanes, machine-guns and submarines – almost all the technology which we think of today as being the tools of modern warfare. But the societies that fought the war were very different from our own.

Europe at the start of the twentieth century was not the closely-knit community it is today. Instead there were bitter rivalries. The continent was divided into two camps, each committed to defending their allies. In one camp were Germany, Austria-Hungary and Italy. In the other were France, Russia and Britain. World War I began because Austria-Hungary and Russia went to war over territory in Eastern Europe, and the other partners in the rival power blocs were dragged into the conflict as a result.

There were other reasons too. Many European countries had colonies – territories in other continents which they controlled and exploited. Although Germany was a very powerful nation, she had few colonies, and was building a large navy to help her gain more territory. Britain, then the richest and most powerful nation on earth, felt threatened by Germany's growing strength.

Many nations, including Britain, feared Germany's growing power. This cartoon shows the German leader, the Kaiser, as 'The Glutton' (greedy eater), trying to consume the world.

The event that 'sparked' World War I was the assassination of the leader of Austria-Hungary, Archduke Franz Ferdinand. The assassin, Gavrilo Princip, was quickly arrested, as shown here, and later died in prison.

POET'S CORNER

John Freeman was a businessman and civil servant by profession, as well as an established poet. Many poems were written in Britain at the outbreak of World War I, but his are the most patriotic and emotional.

The Soldier

Rupert Brooke (1887–1915)

If I should die, think only this of me:
That there's some corner of a foreign field
That is for ever England. There shall be
In that rich earth a richer dust concealed;
A dust whom England bore, shaped, made aware,
Gave, once, her flowers to love, her ways to roam,
A body of England's, breathing English air,
Washed by the rivers, blest by suns of home.
(1914)

concealed
Hidden.

bore
Gave give birth to.

These opening words of 'The Soldier', written in 1914, are among the most famous lines of poetry in the English language. At the time many people found the dignified sentiments of Brooke's poem deeply moving. The poem carries more than a hint of British superiority, with the dust of the poet's English body, lovingly cultured by his nation's countryside, enriching the inferior soil of a foreign land. Although its sentiments may be unfashionable now, it is easy to see how those who lost loved ones in the war would find comfort in its ardent patriotism.

In 1914, poets like Brooke and Freeman could speak of war in heroic and romantic terms. Such sentiments tell us much about people's outlook at this time. The two world wars that scarred the first 50 years of the twentieth century would change these attitudes for ever.

Before 1914, the last great conflict to sweep across Europe was the war against Napoleon a hundred years before. France and Germany had fought each other since, in the Franco-Prussian war of 1870–71, but that conflict lasted less than a year. In Britain the most recent wars had

"FALL IN"
ANSWER NOW
IN YOUR COUNTRY'S
HOUR OF NEED

POET'S CORNER

Handsome and clever, Rupert Brooke was as romantic a figure as his poetry. He knew the British prime minister's family, and even stayed at Downing Street when he was on leave in London. He died young, but his demise was not especially heroic. While sailing to Turkey with the Royal Navy he was bitten by a mosquito and died of blood poisoning. He was buried on the Greek island of Skyros.

Recruitment posters like this generated a huge response in Britain. The army hoped to recruit 100,000 men: 500,000 volunteered in three weeks.

been small-scale colonial skirmishes, where well-trained British soldiers had fought often poorly organised opponents. War was represented in newspapers, novels and children's story books in sporting terms, and seen as a grand adventure.

At the beginning of the war, new recruits were enthusiastic and confident that they would be 'home by Christmas'.

When war broke out in August 1914, all across Europe hundreds of thousands of young men volunteered to fight. Because all other conflicts in living memory had been short, most people believed the war would be over by Christmas.

Death on the Western Front

Sturmangriff (Charge)

August Stramm (1874–1915)

From every corner yelling terror wanting
Shriek
Whips
Life
On
Before
It
Gasping death
The heavens tatter.
Blindly slaughters wild about the horror.
(c.1915)

Dea the Fron

tatter
Tear to shreds.

Written around 1915, this poem captures some of the delirious fear felt by soldiers in the moments when they had to leave the relative safety of their trench and advance towards the enemy. Its stark style contrasts tellingly with the romantic heroism of the previous poems. The reader feels that the poet has experienced these feelings directly. Stramm's innovative, concentrated technique was greatly admired by his fellow German poets, and uses sound and rhythm instead of sentences to convey the horror of battle.

When World War I began, military technology was at a point where the weapons of defence were much better than the weapons of attack. This resulted in more soldiers being killed in the war than in any other previous conflict. In Western Europe, the first stage of the war had seen German armies advance into France. But this advance had been halted, and by late autumn vast lines of opposing trenches – ditches dug to protect soldiers – stretched from Switzerland to the Belgian coast. These trenches were defended very effectively by rows of barbed wire and deadly machine-guns.

The designer of the machine-gun, American Harim Maxim, was advised by a friend to 'invent something that will enable these Europeans to cut each other's throats with greater facility'. He succeeded all too well. Line after line of attacking infantrymen, often laden with over 26kg of equipment, was caught on the barbed wire and mown down like sheaves of corn. The scale of the slaughter was incomprehensible. The war lasted for four terrible years, and on average 5,600 men were killed every day.

POET'S CORNER

Stramm was a captain in the German army. He was killed in an assault similar to the one described in this poem. He wrote vividly about the horrors endured by front-line troops, conveying the terror of shelling, frontal assault and hand-to-hand combat like no other German war poet.

Above: Wounded men waiting to be taken to a casualty clearing station.

Below: 'Over the Top'. Such attacks regularly ended in slaughter as the advancing troops were mown down by machine-gun fire.

Life in the Trenches

Gold Braid

A.A. Milne 1882–1956

Same old trenches, same old view,
Same old rats as blooming tame,
Same old dug-outs, nothing new,
Same old smell, the very same,
Same old bodies out in front,
Same old strafe from two till four,
Same old scratching, same old 'unt,
Same old bloody war.
(1915)

dug-outs
Covered shelters dug into the sides of trenches to provide protection.

strafe
A German word adopted by British troops, meaning heavy fire from machine-guns and rifles.

same old 'unt
The poet means the hunt for lice in his hair and body.

Away from the intense terror of combat, the everyday life of a soldier in the trenches was often very dull. This extract from Milne's poem of 1915 captures this monotony in its repeated verses, listing the everyday miseries endured by front-line troops. They share their accommodation with rats, who are so commonplace they almost seem like pets. They also fight a losing battle against lice – tiny bloodsucking insects that infest their clothing and bodies. Even the horrors of the war – dead bodies left to rot in the no man's land between the trenches – become part of the mindless, numbing routine.

After the first six weeks of conflict, the front line between the German, French and British trenches remained all but the same for almost the rest of the war. German trenches were generally much better maintained. British trenches were much less comfortable. One British officer, George Coppard, recalled, 'The whole conduct of our trench warfare seemed to be based on the concept that we ... were not stopping in the trenches very long, but were tarrying awhile on the way to Berlin'. Because of this, British trenches were usually poorly built, and British soldiers suffered a great deal of discomfort.

The trenches were particularly unpleasant during the winter, when they often filled with water. Men were forced to wade from place to place, knee deep in mud. Those on sentry duty sometimes had to stand waist deep in freezing water for many hours.

Right: Mud and water were a regular torment in the trenches. This trench is too waterlogged for regular use.

Soldiers sleeping in crude dugouts during a lull in the fighting in 1916.

POET'S CORNER

A.A. Milne was a signals officer in the British army during the war. He survived the battle of the Somme, and went on to become one of the most well-known children's authors in the world. His most famous creation is Winnie the Pooh, and he also adapted Kenneth Grahame's book *The Wind in the Willows* for the stage as *Toad of Toad Hall*.

God Heard the Embattled Nations

J.C. Squire 1884–1958

God heard the embattled nations sing and shout:
'Gott straffe England' – 'God save the King' –
'God this' – 'God that' – and 'God the other thing':
'My God,' said God, 'I've got my work cut out.'

(1915)

embattled
Engaged in warfare.

straffe
In this context this German word means 'punish'.

Every nation at the start of the war claimed that God supported it and its cause. Propaganda on all sides depicted the war as a struggle between the forces of Godliness, and a barbaric enemy in league with the devil. Squire cynically imagines God listening to the prayers of both the German and British armies, each of which claims to have Him on its side.

The British general Sir Douglas Haig was responsible for the British attack on the Somme, seen by many historians as the greatest military blunder of the war. Yet before the attack, Haig said: 'I feel every step of my plan has been taken with the Divine help' – meaning that he felt God had helped him plan his battle strategy.

Belief in the Christian God had been widespread in Europe up until the beginning of the nineteenth century. Over the next hundred years, societies changed rapidly. Many people moved from the countryside to the growing towns and cities. Peasants and farm workers became factory hands. Away from the country communities, which had been built around the Church, religion became less important and people's beliefs began to fade. The huge slaughter of World War I, and the horrendous conditions in which it was fought, further undermined people's belief in God. The new philosophy of communism, which many people were

A memorial service attended by South African troops at Delville Wood on the Somme in 1916. All the warring nations relied on front-line priests to bring comfort to their troops.

POET'S CORNER

J.C. Squire was a critic and a poet who was famed for his mocking style. He became literary editor of two very well respected British publications – the *New Statesman* and the *Observer*. He was knighted in 1933.

discovering at that time, also weakened people's religious beliefs. It taught that religion was no more than an escape from the realities of life.

After the war many people turned to the occult rather than Christianity for comfort. 'Mediums', who claimed to be able to talk to the dead, were in great demand from relatives desperate to make contact with a father, brother or son killed in the trenches. Some of these mediums undoubtedly believed they had a gift which enabled them to make contact with the dead, but many were frauds who cynically exploited the mass grieving that followed the war, charging mourning relatives high fees to bring fake messages from 'beyond the grave'.

The Bishop of London speaking in London's Victoria Park, 23 September 1916. Many Christians found their faith severely tested by the events of the Great War.

Munition Wages

Madeline Ida Bedford

Earning high wages? Yus,
Five quid a week.
A woman, too, mind you,
I calls it dim sweet.

We're all here today, mate,
Tomorrow – perhaps dead,
If Fate tumbles on us
And blows up our shed.

Afraid! Are yer kidding?
With money to spend!
Years back I wore tatters,
Now – silk stocking, mi friend!
(c.1916)

Munition
Usually written as 'munitions': military weapons and ammunition.

dim
A polite way of saying damn.

shed
Factory.

tatters
Ragged clothes.

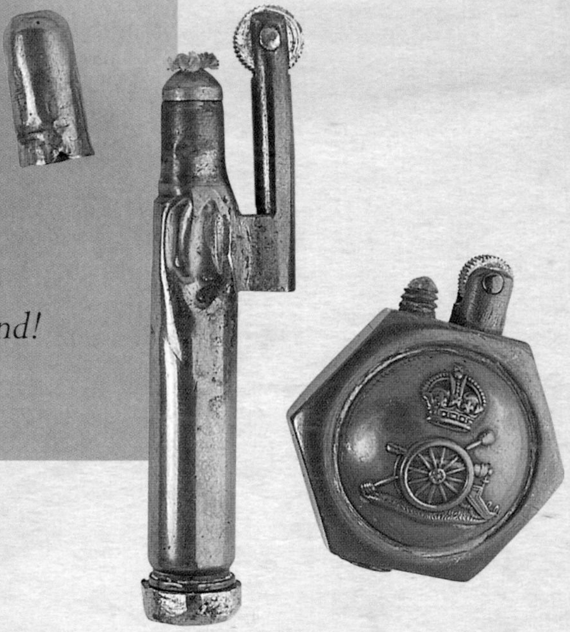

This extract from a friendly, conversational poem, written in the slang, or 'colloquial', voice of a working-class London woman around 1916, is about work in a munitions factory. Such work, making shells and bullets, was highly dangerous. An accident could cause a catastrophic explosion and destroy a factory in seconds. But, says the poet, there are compensations – before the war it was unusual for women to be paid such good wages.

By the winter of 1914, any hope that the war would be over by Christmas had evaporated. The countries involved had to make major changes to their economies. Factories that had once made trams now produced machine-guns. As so many men had left to join the armed forces

POET'S CORNER

This poem originally appeared in a collection of poetry published during the war called *The Young Captain*. Since then it has been published in several anthologies of war poetry. Of Madeline Ida Bedford almost nothing is known, not even the dates of her life.

Women assembling artillery shells in a munitions factory.

THESE WOMEN ARE DOING THEIR BIT
LEARN TO MAKE MUNITIONS

During World War I women were actively encouraged to work in the munitions factories and many other areas of industry, whereas before the war such a situation would have been unthinkable.

there was a labour shortage. In Britain, shells and ammunition were in particularly short supply, so thousands of women began to work in munitions factories. Women also began to do other sorts of 'man's work' which they had never been allowed to do before, such as driving trams, delivering coal and working in offices.

For most of history women had been seen as homemakers and mothers. At the start of the twentieth century they were not even allowed to vote. The war presented a wonderful opportunity for women to prove that they were just as valuable and capable as men. The chance to earn a good wage also allowed women to be much more independent. In Britain women were given the vote in 1918, in recognition of their contribution to the war.

Les Soliloques du Soldat (The Soldier's Soliloquies, I)

Marc De Larreguy De Civrieux (1895–1916)

After the Charleroi affair
And since we waved the Marne goodbye,
I drag my carcass everywhere,
But never know the reason why.

In trench and barn I spend each day,
From fort or attic glimpse the sky,
At this war simply slog away,
But never know the reason why.

I ask, hoping to understand
This slaughter's purpose. The reply
I get is: 'For the Motherland!'
But never know the reason why.

(1916)

soliloquies
A poetic or theatrical term which means speaking to yourself.

Charleroi and Marne
Areas of Belgium and France where heavy fighting between French and German troops occurred.

carcass
Literally a dead body, but here the poet means his weary self.

As the fighting dragged on, troops on all sides grew increasingly weary. In this extract the poet mentions two battles at the start of the war where French soldiers fought bravely to stop the German army overrunning their country. Now, two years later in 1916, the war has reached a stalemate and the exhausted writer wonders why they are still fighting. The trite patriotism of 'For the Motherland!' no longer inspires his weary body.

The French lost more soldiers on the Western Front than any other nation. In the first two weeks of the war 300,000 men were killed or wounded. Dreadful slaughter at battles like Verdun saw French casualties rise to over 5.5 million by the end of the war (1,385,300 of these were killed).

Looking back, many people wonder why soldiers allowed themselves to be led to their deaths in such huge numbers. At the time, most soldiers were obedient to their officers in a way that would be unthinkable in today's less reverential societies. Military discipline at the Front was also very harsh. Cowardice or desertion was punished by firing squad. During attacks, military policemen patrolled the trenches, ready to shoot dead any soldier who did not go over the top when the signal was given.

POET'S CORNER

Marc De Larreguy De Civrieux was barely 21 when he was killed at Verdun in 1916. He wrote several poems about the unthinking patriotism that made the French government carry on fighting.

Troops prepare for an attack. Their courage is boosted by the grim fact that they will be shot by their own officers if they fail to 'go over the top'.

A cartoon depicting the French mutiny in 1917. An officer attempts to inspire his troops, with little success.

Occasionally there were rebellions. In June 1917 half the French army mutinied – the military term for refusing to obey orders. The French authorities acted swiftly. The mutiny was kept secret, and reforms such as more home leave and better rations were introduced. In Russia, mutinous troops cost their country the war. When soldiers refused to carry on fighting the Russians surrendered huge chunks of territory to Germany, and a communist regime seized power.

'Blighters'

Siegfried Sassoon (1886–1967)

The House is crammed: tier beyond tier they grin
And cackle at the Show, while prancing ranks
Of harlots shrill the chorus, drunk with din;
'We're sure the Kaiser loves our dear old Tanks!'

I'd like to see a Tank come down the stalls,
Lurching to rag-time tunes, or 'Home Sweet Home',
And there'd be no more jokes in Music-halls
To mock the riddled corpses round Bapaume.

(1916)

blighter
Early twentieth-century slang for an unpleasant person.

house
Theatre.

tier
A row of seats.

harlot
Literally a prostitute, but in this case the poet means a girl who dances and sings on the stage.

riddled
In this case, full of bullet holes.

Bapaume
French town and scene of heavy fighting between British and German troops during the battle of the Somme.

In this bitter poem, the writer is a soldier home on leave. He visits the music hall, a popular form of entertainment featuring singers, dancers and comedians. He wonders how people can be so light-hearted after all the terrible slaughter he has seen. The poem mentions tanks, introduced to the Western Front for the first time that year. Although they often broke down, they terrified the troops that had to fight them. The poet wonders how the audience would react if a tank lurched into view, and started to grind and clank its way towards them.

During the war, people at home knew little of the terrible realities of combat. While soldiers were living in dreadful discomfort, and being slaughtered in their thousands every day, newspapers and newsreels (cinema news programmes) continued to present the war as a great adventure. This biased presentation of news (propaganda) on the home front also led to a jeering hatred of all things German. In Britain, shops with German names were ransacked, and even dachshund dogs (a German breed) were stoned on the street.

Soldiers on leave rarely spoke about the day-to-day horrors they faced in the trenches. Many felt they did not want to distress their relatives. Only the mounting casualty lists told the real story. Writer Robert Graves found the attitudes of the home population so repellent that after one trip home he wrote, 'Once more I felt glad to be back in the trenches'.

A British tank in action on the Western Front.

Below: Soldiers at home for Christmas in 1916. While many were glad of the chance to visit their homes and families, others felt only anger at the ignorance of civilians to the realities of the war.

POET'S CORNER

Siegfried Sassoon, an infantry officer on the Western Front, was the first British war poet to write poetry that criticised the war. He came from an upper-class family, and fought with exceptional bravery, which probably protected him from being punished for being so outspoken.

THE END OF IDEALISM

Dulce et Decorum est

Wilfred Owen (1893–1918)

As under a green sea I saw him drowning…

If in some smothering dreams you too could pace
Behind the wagon that we flung him in,
And watch the white eyes writhing in his face,
His hanging face, like a devil's sick of sin…

My friend, you would not tell with such high zest
To children ardent for some desperate glory,
The old Lie: Dulce et decorum est
Pro patria mori.

(1917)

smothering
Suffocating.

zest
Enthusiasm.

ardent
Eager.

Dulce et decorum est pro patria mori
This Latin phrase means 'It is sweet and honourable to die for one's country'.

In this extract from one of the most famous poems of the war, Owen describes in merciless detail the horrific suffering of a young soldier who has been gassed. He contrasts this nightmarish scene with the naïve, unthinking patriotism of young men who have rushed to join the army. He finishes the poem by quoting a phrase from the Roman poet Horace, which would have been familiar to many soldiers from their schooldays.

Silent and sinister, gas was one of the many new weapons of World War I. Although it was often fatal, it was intended to disable and demoralise rather than kill. First used by Germany in 1915, but swiftly followed by France and Britain, gas killed thousands of soldiers and left thousands more with lungs and eyes so badly damaged they would never recover. At first, gas was

The End of Idealism

unleashed from canisters, and blew across no man's land with the wind. But winds could change, blowing it back to the soldiers who had released it. Gas-filled shells were a more reliable way of delivering this weapon, and by the end of the war one in four shells carried gas rather than high explosives.

POET'S CORNER

Wilfred Owen, who was a British officer on the Western Front, wrote, 'My subject is war and the pity of war'. He is generally regarded as Britain's greatest war poet. To read his poems is to marvel at how someone of such intense sensitivity and compassion could cope with the day-to-day horror of the war.

Above: A German infantryman, protected by his gas mask, about to hurl a gas bomb while his comrade prepares to hand him another.

Below: British troops blinded in a gas attack line up for treatment, although there was little that the medicine of the time could do to help them.

An Irish Airman Foresees his Death

W.B. Yeats (1865–1939)

I know that I shall meet my fate
Somewhere among the clouds above;
Those that I fight I do not hate,
Those that I guard I do not love . . .
. . . I balanced all, brought all to mind,
The years to come seemed waste of breath,
A waste of breath the years behind
In balance with this life, this death.
(1922)

fate
The poet means his death.

This extract from Yeats' popular poem concerns the private thoughts of a pilot as he thinks about his inevitable death in combat. He has no quarrel with the Germans and no great loyalty to Britain, for whom he is fighting. At the time Ireland was part of the United Kingdom, and many Irish people, particularly in the south of the country, wanted Ireland to be independent. At the end of the poem Yeats imagines the pilot reviewing his life, dismissing both his past and future, and accepting his end with a moving dignity.

In a war characterised by massively inglorious machine-gun slaughter, sinister poisonous gas and anonymous artillery bombardments, pilots were seen as glamorous, romantic figures, taking part in one-to-one combat, like medieval knights, with their opponents in the skies. But the life of a front-line fighter pilot was usually brief. There were 22,000 pilots in the British Royal Flying Corps during the war, and over half of them were killed.

POET'S CORNER

William Butler Yeats was one of Ireland's greatest writers, winning the Nobel Prize for Literature in 1923. He wrote this poem for a family friend, Major Gregory, an Irish pilot killed in the war. Yeats was nearly 50 when war broke out, and did not fight. This was his only poem about the war.

Left: This painting by Dudley Tennant shows British and German fighter planes in combat during 1918.

Below: Manfred von Richthofen (1892–1918), the greatest German air ace of World War I, shown here (centre) with other members of his squadron and his dog, Moritz. Richthofen shot down 80 Allied aircraft before being killed himself in action. His nickname, the Red Baron, referred to the colour of his plane.

World War I completely transformed people's perceptions of aeroplanes. After the first successful powered flight in 1907 they were seen as a wonderful novelty. But in the brief four years of World War I, they were transformed from flimsy reconnaissance spotters to fighter planes and heavy bombers, capable of flying to enemy cities and dropping bombs on civilian populations hundreds of kilometres away from the actual fighting.

Troopship: mid-Atlantic

Wilfrid Gibson (1878–1962)

Boys from the Middle West lounge listlessly
In the unlanthorned darkness, boys who go,
Beckoned by some unchallengeable dream,
To unknown lands to fight an unknown foe.
(1917)

Middle West
The central part of the United States.

listlessly
Lacking enthusiasm.

unlanthorned
Unlit.

beckoned
Called forward.

This extract is part of a poem written by Wilfrid Gibson when he was aboard a troopship in July 1917, with some of the first American soldiers to come to Europe. The United States has recently joined the war on the side of Britain and France, but the American soldiers crossing the Atlantic to fight are uncertain. Their country has high ideals, but they know nothing of the countries they will be risking their lives to defend, and just as little about the Germans they will be fighting.

American president Woodrow Wilson kept the United States out of the war for over two years, although American factories provided Britain and other fighting nations with arms and supplies. At first, like many Americans, Wilson felt his country should not send men to fight. As the war went on he changed his mind, but did not want to bring the United States into the war unwillingly.

Los Angeles Examiner

VOL. XIV—NO. 113 Official Forecast—Cloudy TUESDAY LOS ANGELES, APRIL 3, 1917. PRICE TWO CENTS TELEPHONES—MAIN 8300, HOME 10196

WAR! SAYS WILSON; BIG ARMY WANTED

FIRST OF U.S.ARMED SHIPS IS 'U' VICTIM

LATEST EARLY MORNING NEWS

500,000 MEN NEEDED AT ONCE; AID TO ALLIES WITHOUT LIMIT

President Calls on Congress to Throw All Nation's Resources Against German Autocracy

Here Is American Congress War Declaration Resolution

CONGRESS RALLIES TO STIRRING PLEA OF NATION'S CHIEF

Amid Scenes of Wild Enthusiasm President Advises 'State of War' Declaration and Men, Ships and Money to Crush 'Foe of Liberty'

After Wilson decided the United States would join the war, recruitment began in earnest, as this front page from the Los Angeles Examiner *of 3 April 1917 shows.*

In the years before the war millions of people had emigrated to the United States from Europe. Many were from Germany and did not want their new country to fight against their former homeland. Other newly-arrived immigrants felt they had fled from Europe partly to get away from wars such as this one.

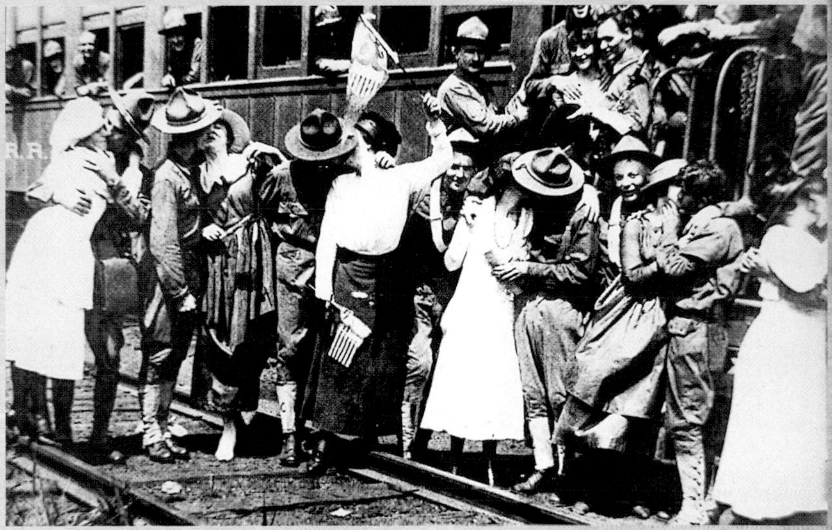
American soldiers of the 62nd Regiment kiss their girls goodbye as they leave for Europe.

In January 1917 Germany decided to sink any ship it could find in British waters. American passenger and cargo ships were attacked and this turned people in the United States against Germany. Wilson declared war in April 1917. It took a year for the United States' troops to be trained and transported over the Atlantic, but by the end of the war there were 2 million American soldiers fighting in France. The arrival of these fresh troops to help the exhausted French and British was crucial to the eventual defeat of Germany.

POET'S CORNER

Wilfrid Gibson was a close friend of Rupert Brooke. He wrote many poems, and his most common subject was the plight of the ordinary citizen caught up in the great events of history.

THE COST OF THE WAR

Disabled

Wilfred Owen (1893–1918)

He sat in a wheeled chair, waiting for dark,
And shivered in his ghastly suit of grey,
Legless, sewn short at elbow.

One time he liked a bloodsmear down his leg,
After the matches, carried shoulder high.
It was after football, when he'd drunk a peg,
He thought he'd better join...

Some cheered him home,
but not as crowds cheer Goal.
Only a solemn man who brought him fruits
Thanked *him; and then inquired about his soul.*

To-night he noticed how the women's eyes
Passed from him
to the strong men that were whole.
How cold and late it is! Why don't they come
And put him into bed? Why don't they come?
(1918)

peg
A glass of whisky.

This extract, from one of Wilfred Owen's most poignant poems, pictures a maimed, legless soldier, alone at dusk by a hospital window. He is so helpless he must rely on the nurses to prepare him for bed. In the poem, the soldier, a former athlete, hears the hue and cry of a football game in the distance, and remembers his own glory days. Now he is home, but the crowds that greeted his hospital ship were subdued. Owen wrote this poem in 1918 while in hospital in Edinburgh, where he would have met such wounded soldiers.

For families in all the warring nations, the relief of having a father or brother survive the war was sometimes short lived. Many men came home to die a long, lingering death from injuries received in battle.

If you escaped service without injury, unemployment was often waiting. Here unemployed officers, wearing masks to protect their anonymity, play a barrel organ in London in 1920 to try to raise money for their families.

The war left millions wounded. In Britain alone a quarter of those who had served as soldiers were injured badly enough to qualify for a government disability pension. Although many of these men were able to live normal lives, there were tens of thousands who had been severely injured. Some, like the soldier in this poem, had lost both legs. Others had lost both arms, or had been blinded or had their lungs ruined by gas.

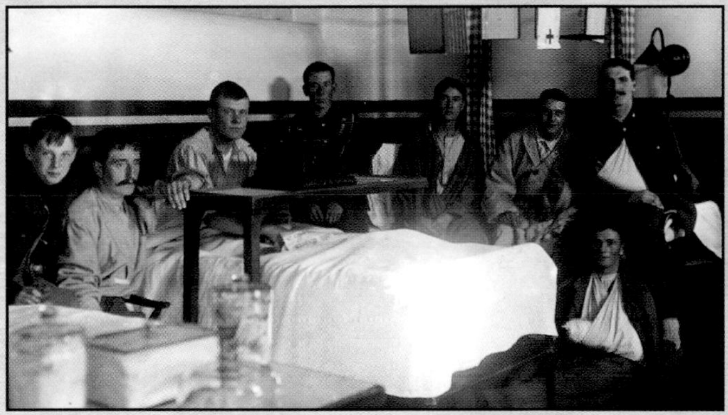

Wounded soldiers in a London hospital.

The dreadful experiences of many soldiers in the trenches led to mental illness too, known at the time as 'shell shock'. Such men required many years of patient care before they could face the world again. Some historians estimate that the war left a quarter of a million men throughout Europe suffering from shell shock.

POET'S CORNER

Owen was an outstanding soldier and was awarded a Military Cross for exceptional bravery. He was killed in France seven days before the war ended. His parents received a telegram telling them of his death as church bells were ringing in celebration on the day peace was declared.

Reconciliation

Siegfried Sassoon (1886–1967)

When you are standing at your hero's grave,
Or near some homeless village where he died,
Remember, through your heart's rekindling pride,
The German soldiers who were loyal and brave.

Men fought like brutes; and hideous things were done;
And you have nourished hatred, harsh and blind.
But in that Golgotha perhaps you'll find
The mothers of the men who killed your son.
(1918)

rekindling
Stirring again.

nourished
Encouraged.

Golgotha
The place where Christ died – here Sassoon means a place of great suffering.

Sassoon's moving poem of 1918 pictures the mothers of dead soldiers visiting the battlegrounds where their sons were killed. He asks them to spare a thought for the German soldiers who also died in battle. He acknowledges that there was brutality and hatred on both sides, but asks these grieving women to recognise that there are German mothers who are suffering too.

The war ended on 11 November 1918. Germany had beaten Russia and gained much territory on her eastern border. But her exhausted armies in the west were finally driven back to Germany by the French, British and American armies, and the German government was forced to surrender. The human cost of the war was astronomical. In France, for example, over half the men aged between 20 and 35 had been killed or wounded. Overall, at least 10 million soldiers died, and another 20 million were wounded.

Armistice and Beyond

Siegfried Sassoon's plea for forgiveness and reconciliation fell mainly on deaf ears. The war was settled with the Versailles Peace Conference, and Germany was punished severely. Territory was taken from it, and it was made to pay 'reparations' – compensation to the nations it had fought.

This caused a great deal of bitterness in Germany, which was exploited by Adolf Hitler and the Nazi party. They seized power in 1933, determined to take revenge for the wrongs they felt had been visited on Germany. This led directly to World War II – an even greater, more terrible conflict, which was to claim over four times as many lives.

POET'S CORNER

Sassoon survived the war and his poetry brought him national fame. He also published two classic autobiographies: *Memoirs of a Fox-Hunting Man* and *Memoirs of an Infantry Officer*. He met Wilfred Owen while on sick leave in Edinburgh. He encouraged him to write more poetry, and the two men became good friends.

Above: Soldiers celebrate Armistice Day, 11 November 1918.

Below: Veterans of the Great War in London on Remembrance Sunday, 1999.

GLOSSARY

Difficult words from the verse appear alongside each poem. This glossary explains words used in the main text. The page numbers are given so that you can study the glossary and then see how the words have been used.

ardent *(p. 6) Eager, often unthinkingly or unquestioningly so.*

biased *(p. 18) Presenting only one side of an argument or view of events.*

communism *(p. 13) A political belief in which the state controls the wealth and industry of a country on behalf of the people.*

evoke *(p. 4) To conjure up a feeling or image.*

exploit *(p. 5) Make use of, often unfairly.*

'go over the top' *(p. 17) A phrase used by troops during the war to mean to charge against the enemy. To do this they had to 'go over the top' of their trenches and into no man's land.*

hue and cry *(p. 26) A loud noise made by a crowd.*

infantrymen *(pp. 9, 21) Soldiers belonging to a regiment of foot-soldiers.*

innovative *(p. 8) Daringly new and experimental.*

Military Cross *(p. 27) A medal awarded to British soldiers for outstanding bravery.*

mutiny *(p. 17) A revolt in the armed services, usually when men refuse to obey orders.*

naïve *(p. 20) Over-trusting; a tendency to believe something without questioning it.*

no man's land *(pp. 10, 21) The space between two opposing armies. On the Western Front this was the shell-torn landscape between the Allied and German trenches.*

patriotic *(p. 4) Having a deep love and loyalty for one's country.*

perceptions *(p. 23) Opinions and ideas.*

power blocs *(p. 5) Groups of countries that have joined together to defend their mutual interests against a common enemy.*

pride *(p. 4) A sense of one's own worth compared to others.*

propaganda *(pp. 12, 18) Biased news and information put out by a government to convince its citizens that a particular viewpoint or policy is right.*

reconnaissance *(p. 23) A survey of enemy positions and strength.*

repellent *(p. 19) Deeply unpleasant or disgusting.*

romantic *(pp. 6, 7, 22) Unrealistically glamorous.*

sacrifice *(p. 4) To give up something precious, especially one's own life, for a worthwhile cause.*

sentiment *(p. 6) A deeply felt idea.*

strategy *(p. 12) The art of moving troops, ships, aircraft etc. into favourable positions.*

tarry *(p. 11) To remain, linger.*

trenches *(pp. 8, 10, 11, 17, 19) Lines of ditches, fortified by sandbags and barbed wire, which soldiers dug to protect themselves and defend their positions.*

trite *(p. 16) Stale or meaningless, as a result of overuse.*

veterans *(p. 29) Soldiers who have fought in a particular war.*

Western Front *(p. 8) The main battleground in western Europe, stretching from the Belgian coast to Switzerland.*

Books to Read

For younger readers

A Children's English History in Verse
by Kenneth Baker (ed.)
(Faber, 1999)

Armistice 1918
by Reg Grant
(Hodder Wayland, 2000)

Faber Book of War Poetry
by Kenneth Baker (ed.)
(Faber, 1996)

General Haig: Butcher or War Winner?
by Josh Brooman
(Longman, 1998)

In Flanders Field: The Story of the Poem
by Linda Granfield
(Stoddart, 2000)

Some Corner of a Foreign Field
by James Bentley (ed.)
(Little, Brown and Co., 1992)

The War in the Trenches
by Ole Steen Hansen
(Hodder Wayland, 2000)

For older readers

Death's Men
by Dennis Winter
(Penguin Books, 1978)

The First World War
by A.J.P. Taylor
(Penguin Books, 1966)

The Great War and Modern Memory
by Paul Fussell
(Oxford University Press, 2000)

The Lost Voices of World War One
by Tim Cross
(Bloomsbury, 1988)

Up the Line to Death
by Brian Gardner (ed.)
(Methuen, 1964)

INDEX

Numbers in **bold** refer to pictures and captions.